Sacred Stories and Songs

8 ORIGINAL PIANO SOLOS INSPIRED BY THE BIBLE

By Glenda Austin, ~~~~~~~~~, Carolyn Miller, and Jason Sifford

ISBN 978-1-70511-390-5

WILLIS MUSIC

EXCLUSIVELY DISTRIBUTED BY

Hal•Leonard®

Visit Hal Leonard Online at
www.halleonard.com

Contact us:
Hal Leonard
7777 West Bluemound Road
Milwaukee, WI 53213
Email: info@halleonard.com

In Europe, contact:
Hal Leonard Europe Limited
42 Wigmore Street
Marylebone, London, W1U 2RN
Email: info@halleonardeurope.com

In Australia, contact:
Hal Leonard Australia Pty. Ltd.
4 Lentara Court
Cheltenham, Victoria, 3192 Australia
Email: info@halleonard.com.au

NOTES FROM THE COMPOSERS

The Pharaoh's Daughter

Growing up, I always loved the story of how baby Moses was found and brought up by the daughter of the pharaoh. This piece should fit your fingers nicely: hover over the notes in five-finger position and you'll find that you don't have to move very much and can focus on reading the notes and singing along. Listen closely for the change in sound from the verse to the chorus: minor to major!

–Glenda Austin

"A" Is for Apple

Avoid the temptation to guess where your fingers go. If you need a little help finding your starting places, listen carefully to the lyrics. Sometimes the answers are right in front of you if you look for them.

–Jason Sifford

Noah and the Ark

Who doesn't love animals? What's your favorite? Imagine them all marching into that huge ark: lions and tigers and boas, oh my! Be sure you play the eighth notes "swinging" and not as a straight rhythm. You should feel and hear a jazzy sound. Sing along once you have mastered playing it. You will be accompanying yourself at the piano!

–Glenda Austin

Song of Ruth

This song celebrates a wonderful friendship. Performing it will help you develop clear legato and staccato playing. Share your performance with your best friend.

–Randall Hartsell

Daniel in the Lions' Den

It is fun to sing the words as you play. Do you know what the line under the note means in measure 25? How many fermatas can you find? What does *molto rit.* mean? How should the last note be played?

–Carolyn Miller

Let My People Go

Play this piece boldly. It celebrates the bravery of Moses. Have fun dramatically increasing the dynamic contrast between your hands. To the teacher: this piece encourages hand independence and coordination.

–Randall Hartsell

Joseph's Dreams

There are three different dreams in this solo. Find where each one starts. What is different about measures 17 and 33? How does the last chord make you feel?

–Carolyn Miller

Esther's Plea

The story of Esther teaches us an important lesson about inner strength. No matter how difficult a challenge may be, patience and persistence are your greatest allies.

–Jason Sifford

CONTENTS

The Pharaoh's Daughter

This is the miraculous story of a mysterious baby found floating down the river Nile...

Words and Music by
Glenda Austin

Moderately, mysteriously

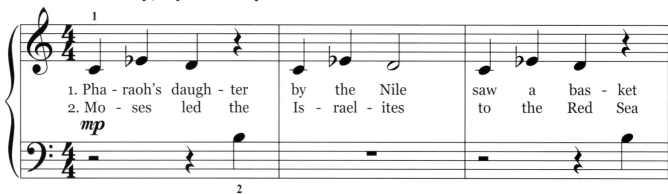

1. Pha - raoh's daugh - ter   by   the   Nile   saw   a   bas - ket
2. Mo - ses   led   the   Is - rael - ites   to   the   Red   Sea

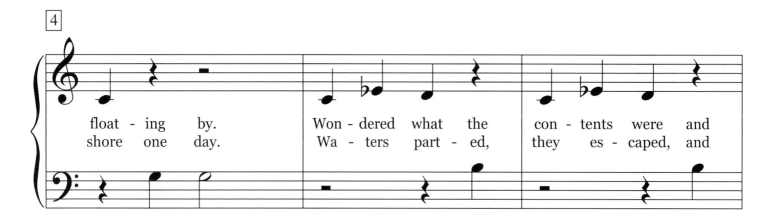

float - ing   by.   Won - dered   what   the   con - tents   were   and
shore   one   day.   Wa - ters   part - ed,   they   es - caped,   and

Accompaniment (Student plays one octave higher than written.)

Moderately, mysteriously

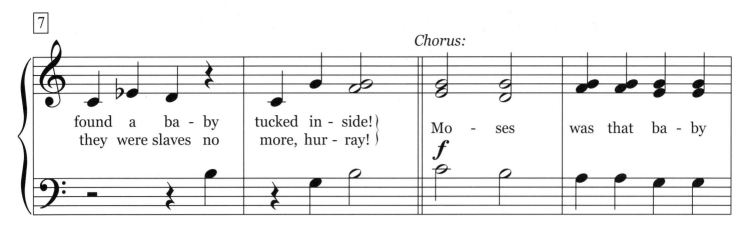

5

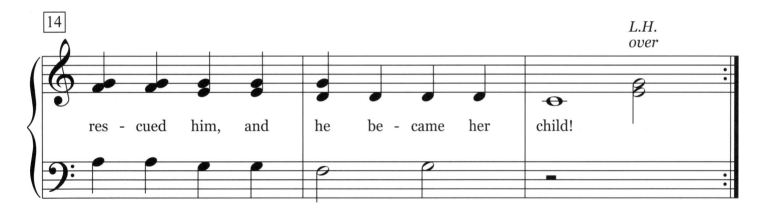

"A" Is for Apple

"The serpent deceived me, and I ate." -Genesis 3:13

Words and Music by
Jason Sifford

Accompaniment (Student plays one octave higher than written.)

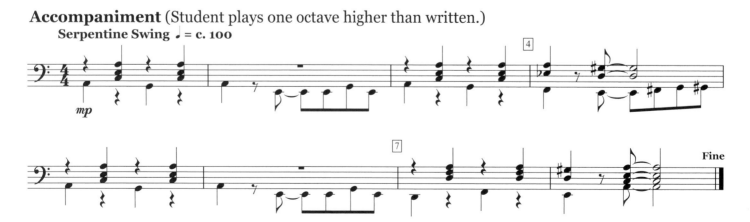

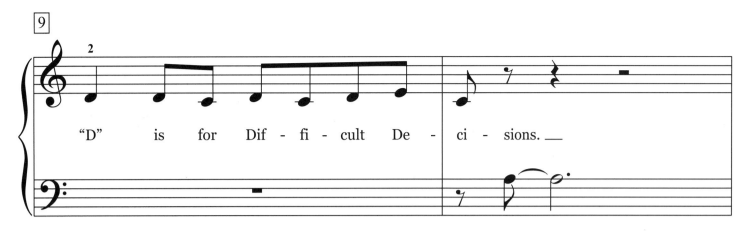

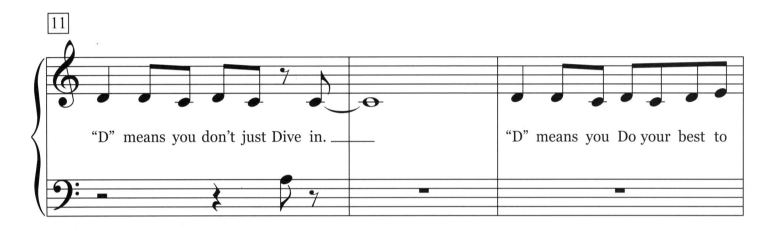

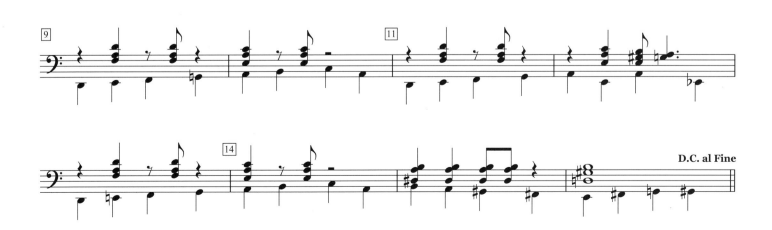

Noah and the Ark

A great flood once covered the earth. This story tells of how the animals were saved!

Words and Music by
Glenda Austin

With a bounce and a swing!

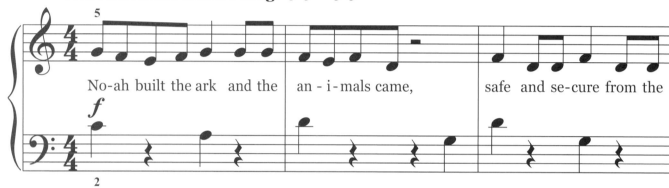

No-ah built the ark and the   an - i - mals came,   safe and se-cure from the

floods   and   rain. There were   birds and dogs and   snails and cats,

Accompaniment (Student plays one octave higher than written.)

With a bounce and a swing!

Song of Ruth

"Your people will be my people and your God my God." -Ruth 1:16

Words and Music by
Randall Hartsell

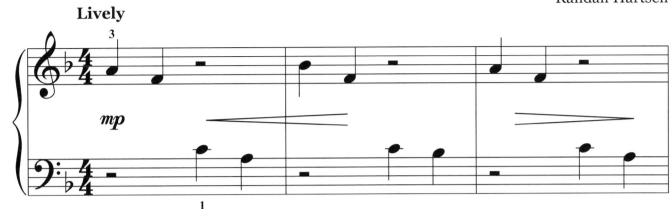

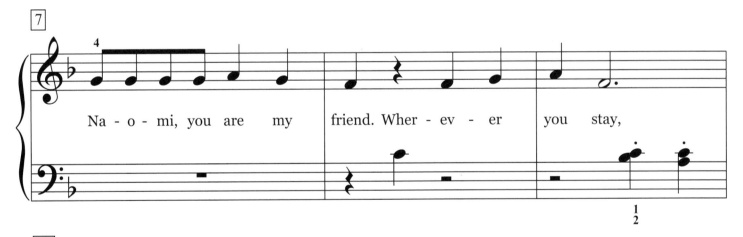

12

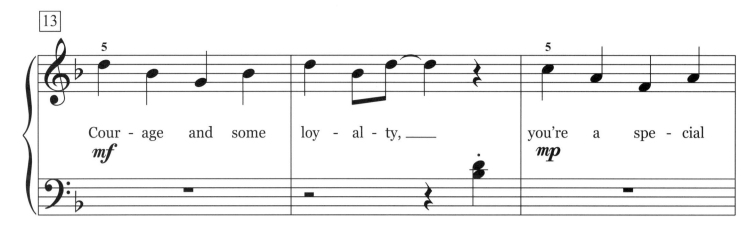

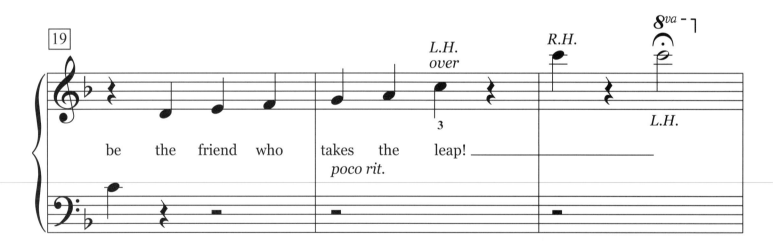

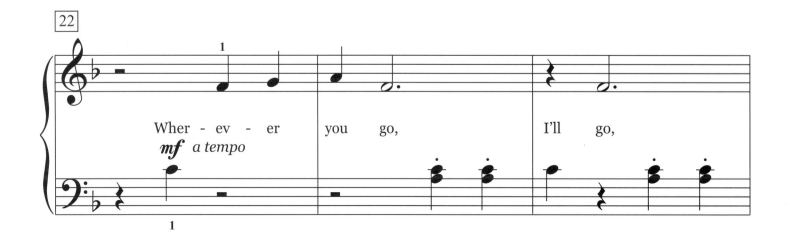

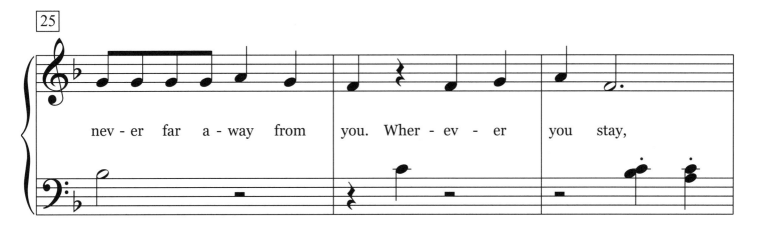

nev - er far a - way from you. Wher - ev - er you stay,

I'll stay. You will al - ways be, ___ You will al - ways be, ___

You will al - ways be my friend.

Daniel in the Lions' Den

This is the story of a brave man who put his complete trust in God.

Words and Music by
Carolyn Miller

15

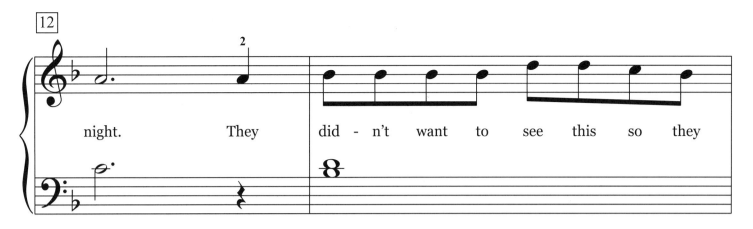

night. They did-n't want to see this so they

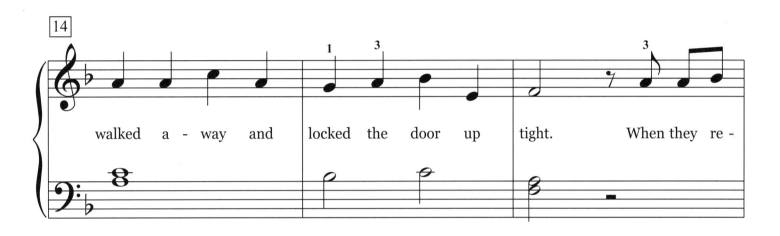

walked a - way and locked the door up tight. When they re -

turned the ver - y next morn - ing, they found Dan - iel sit -ting in the

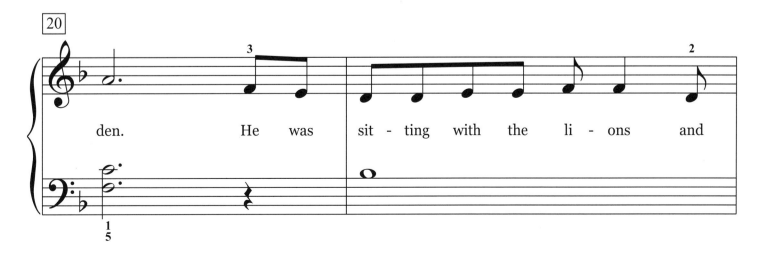

den. He was sit - ting with the li - ons and

16

talk - ing to them, too, and they weren't quite sure what

they should do. So they pulled him out and ___

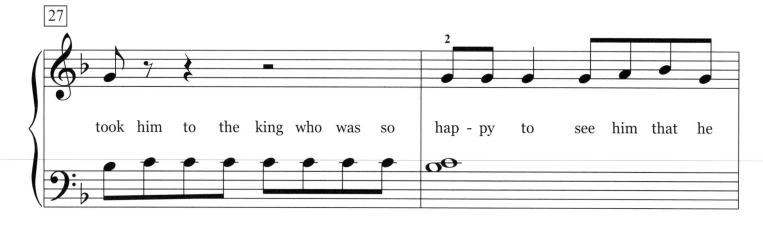

took him to the king who was so hap - py to see him that he

want - ed to sing! Dan - iel told him how an an - gel came to

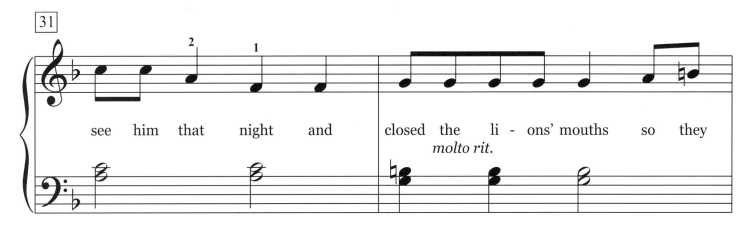

see him that night and closed the li - ons' mouths so they

molto rit.

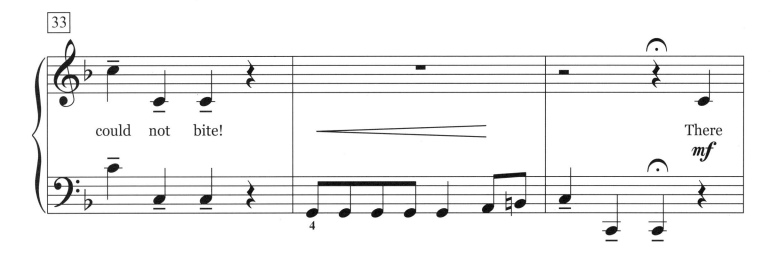

could not bite! There

mf

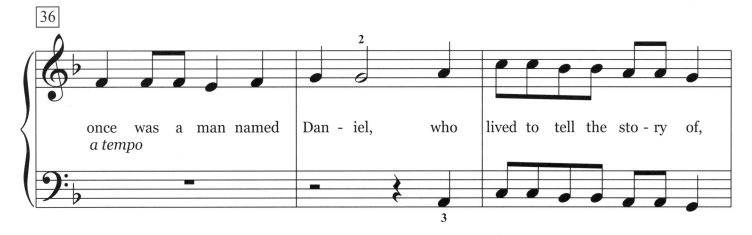

once was a man named Dan - iel, who lived to tell the sto - ry of,

a tempo

lived to tell the sto - ry of a night in the li - ons' den. *f*

8ᵛᵇ

Let My People Go

"Let my people go, so that they may worship me." -Exodus 8:1

Words and Music by
Randall Hartsell

Tell old Pha-raoh, let my peo-ple go.

Free-dom, free-dom for God's peo-ple.

mp

Tell old Pha-raoh, let my peo-ple go.

mf

Let my peo-ple go!

mp

ff poco rit.

Joseph's Dreams

Joseph would tell people what their dreams meant.
Sometimes the results were happy and sometimes sad.

Carolyn Miller

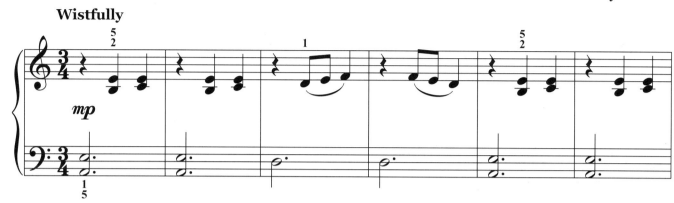

For Esther Houghtaling

Esther's Plea

"For how can I bear to see disaster fall on my people?
How can I bear to see the destruction of my family?" -Esther 8:6

Jason Sifford

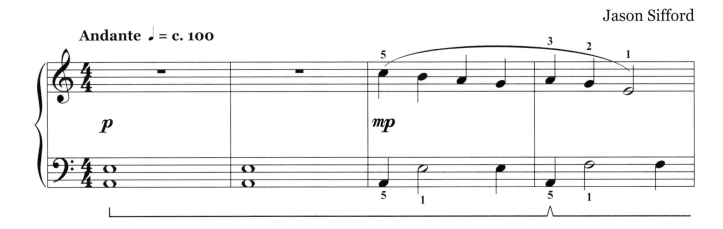

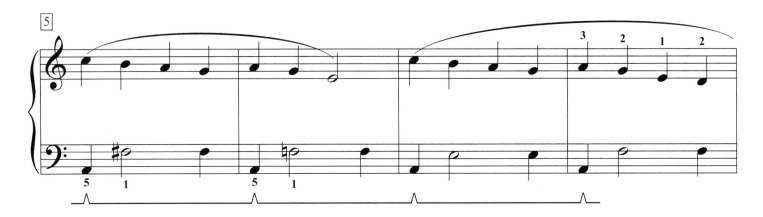

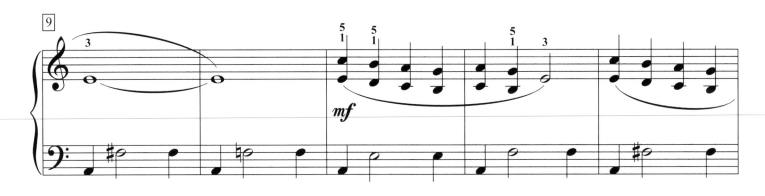

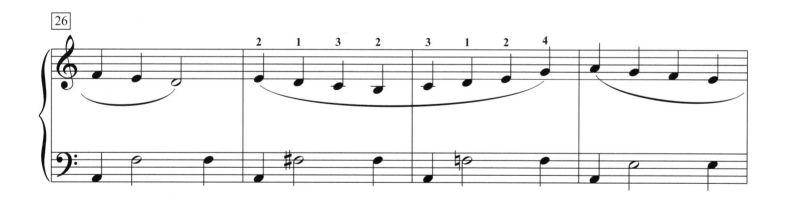

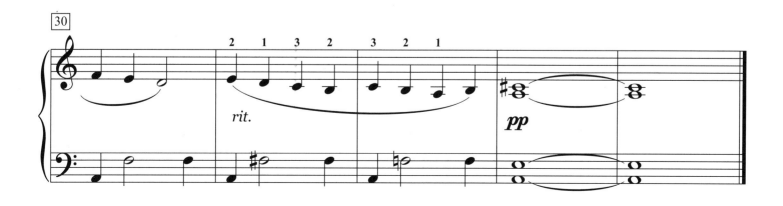

COMPOSER BIOS

Glenda Austin

Glenda is from Joplin, Missouri, and has been a church musician all her life. When she's away from her piano, she enjoys walking, talking, a little bit of cooking, and not having to set an early alarm. Find her on YouTube to view videos of her performing her music!

Randall Hartsell

Randall is a pianist and composer who lives in Charlotte, North Carolina and loves tending to his garden. You can see pictures of his lovely garden on Facebook but look for his music channel on YouTube!

Carolyn Miller

Carolyn lives in Cincinnati, Ohio and enjoys composing pieces for her students. In her spare time she directs a church choir and enjoys spending time with her grandchildren. Subscribe to her YouTube page at Carolyn Miller Piano Music.

Jason Sifford

Jason lives in Iowa City, where he teaches a wonderful group of devoted students, performs regularly with immensely talented local artists, and composes music for his inner child. You can also find Jason on YouTube, or at **www.jasonsifford.com**.